The Lovable Lever

Julie Murray

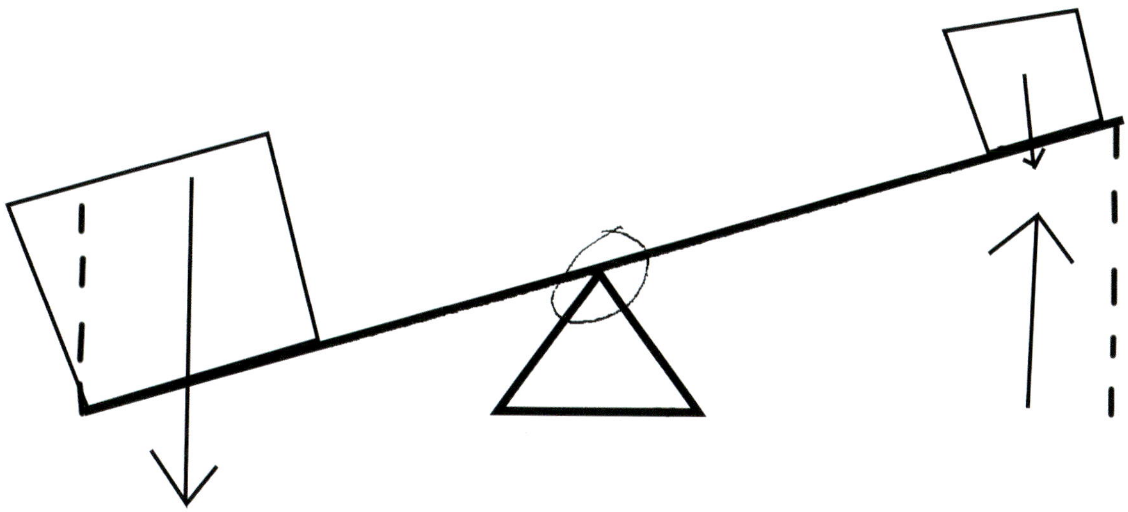

Abdo Kids Junior
is an Imprint of Abdo Kids
abdobooks.com

Abdo Kids
SIMPLE MACHINES

abdobooks.com

Published by Abdo Kids, a division of ABDO, P.O. Box 398166, Minneapolis, Minnesota 55439.

Abdo Kids Junior™ is a trademark and logo of Abdo Kids.

Printed in the United States of America, North Mankato, Minnesota.

052024

092024

THIS BOOK CONTAINS RECYCLED MATERIALS

Photo Credits: Alamy, Getty Images, Shutterstock

Production Contributors: Teddy Borth, Jennie Forsberg, Grace Hansen

Design Contributors: Candice Keimig, Pakou Moua

Library of Congress Control Number: 2023948552

Publisher's Cataloging-in-Publication Data

Names: Murray, Julie, author.

Title: The lovable lever / by Julie Murray

Description: Minneapolis, Minnesota : Abdo Kids, 2025 | Series: Simple machines | Includes online resources and index.

Identifiers: ISBN 9798384900603 (lib. bdg.) | ISBN 9798384901303 (ebook) | ISBN 9798384901655 (Read-to-me eBook)

Subjects: LCSH: Simple machines--Juvenile literature. | Levers--Juvenile literature. | Hinges--Juvenile literature. | Machinery--Juvenile literature. | Hand tools--Juvenile literature.

Classification: DDC 621.8--dc23

Table of Contents

The Lovable Lever

A lever is a simple machine.

It is used to move or
lift a **load**.

All the parts of a lever work together.

A **load** is at one end.

It is what needs moving.

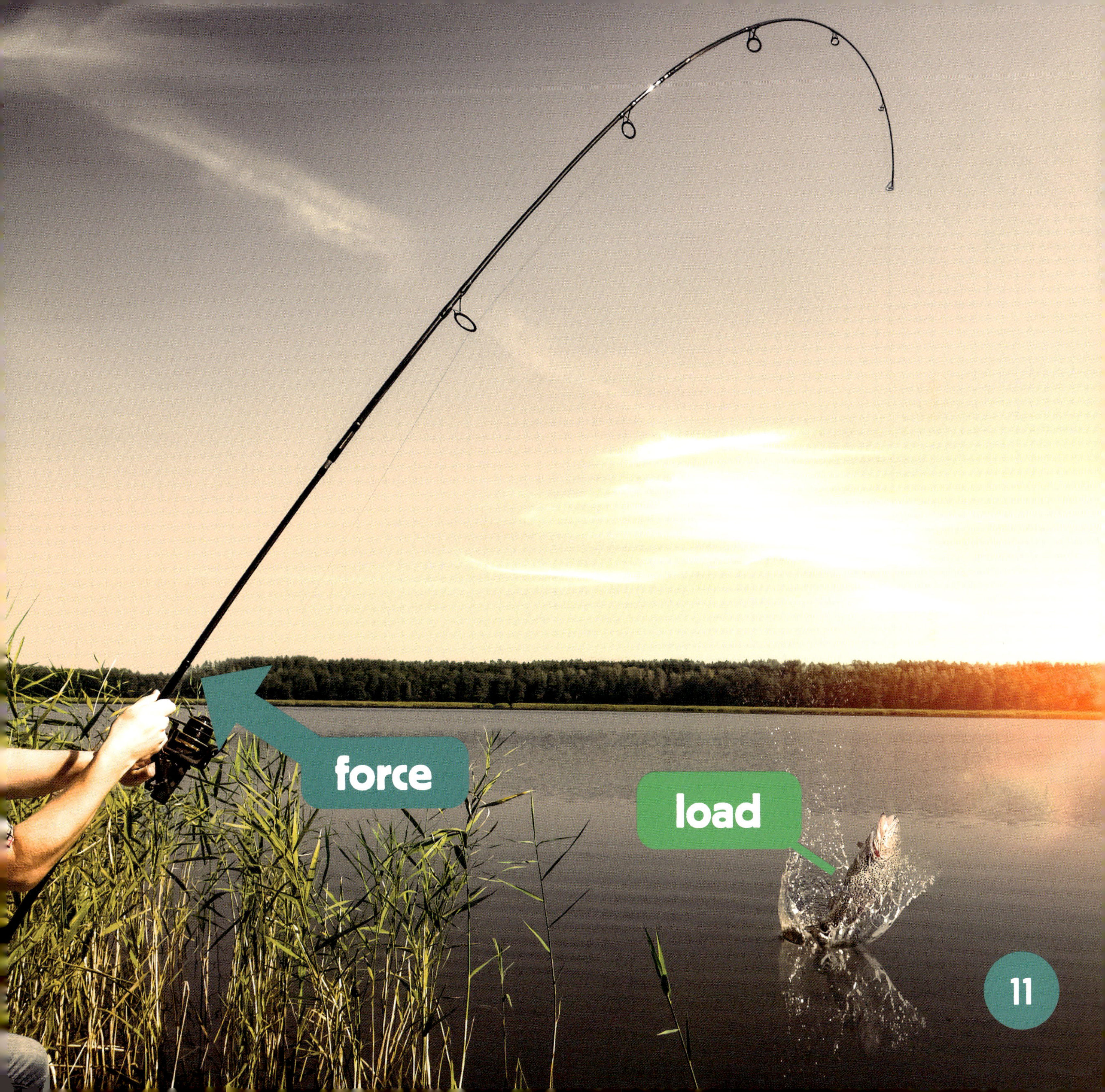
force
load

A bar is under the **load**.

It will lift the load.

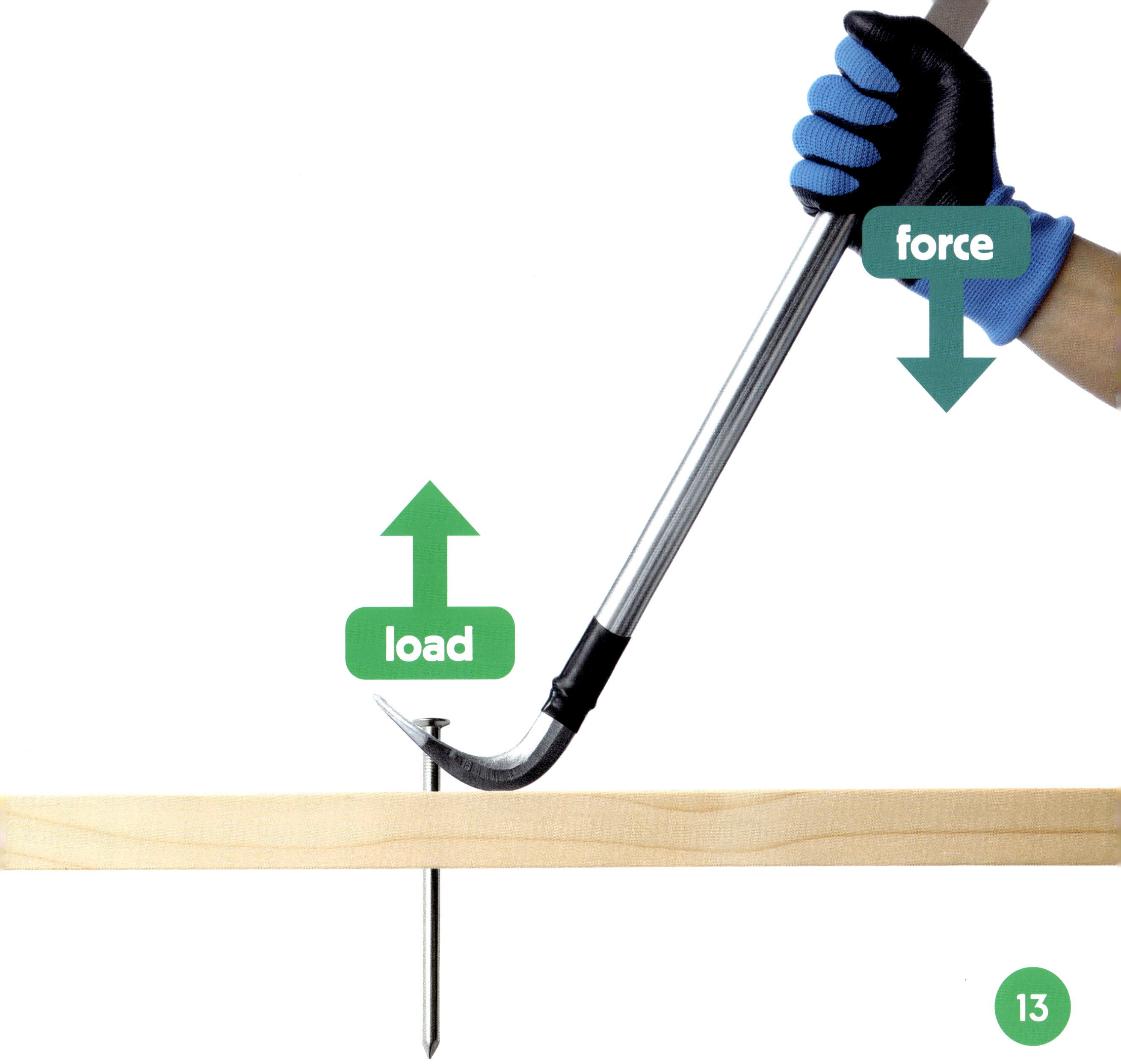
force
load

A **fulcrum** supports the bar.

load
fulcrum
force

Force is needed. It is placed on the other end of the bar.

force
fulcrum
load
force

The **force** moves the **load**.

force
load
fulcrum

A lever makes moving a **load** easier!

load
force
fulcrum

Levers Around You

baseball bat

broom

chopsticks

crowbar

Glossary

force
power, energy, or physical strength.

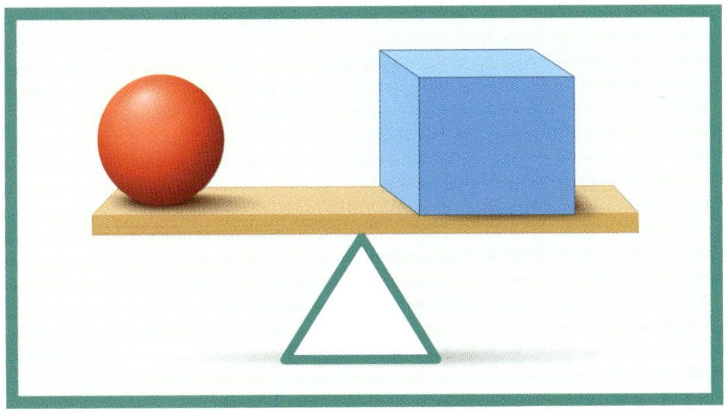

fulcrum
the point of support on which a lever turns.

load
an amount of something carried.

Index